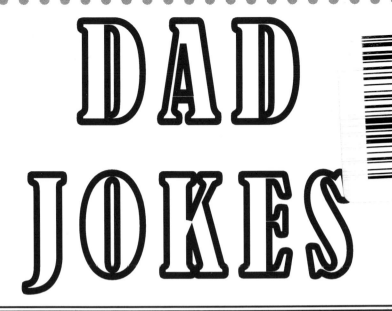

DAD JOKES

TERRIBLY GOOD DAD JOKES

1. What is the best time to go to the dentist?

a.   *Tooth-hurty!*

2. How did the camping trip go?

a.   *It was in tents*

3. **Why did the pony ask for a glass of water?**

a. *Because he was a little horse!*

4. **What does a spy wear on his feet?**

a. *Sneakers.*

5. **Why was the little cookie sad?**

a. *Because his dad was a wafer so long.*

6. Why does Dad not take soccer seriously?

a. *Because he's just doing it for the kicks.*

7. Where is the best place to work if you only have one leg?

a.   IHOP!

8.   Why did Dad have to take a break from hauling shellfish?

a.   Because he pulled a mussel!

9. **Why are books about anti-gravity the best?**

a. *Because they're impossible to put down*

10. **How do you get a tissue to dance?**

a. *Put a little boogie in it!*

11. **What do you call a fish with no eyes?**

a. *A fsh!*

12. **Why did dad quit his job at the shoe recycling shop?**

a. *Because it was sole-destroying.*

13. **Why did the dad not like sushi?**

a. *Because it smelled a little fishy!*

14. **How much do you pay for dead batteries?**

a. *Nothing, they're free of charge!*

15. **What did the sea say to the beach?**

a. *Nothing, it just waved!*

16. **What does a house wear to a nice party?**

a. *A dress.*

17.   Why did the dad take a while to decide on a haircut?

a.   Because he had to mullet over.

18.   Why should you never buy anything with Velcro?

a.   Because it's a total rip-off

19. **Why did the dad not trust stairs?**

a. Because they are always up to something.

20. **How did the dad feel when he found out about the rotation of the earth?**

a. It really made his day!

21. **What do you call a man who murders breakfast food?**

a. *A cereal killer.*

22. **Why is Tinker Bell always in the air?**

a. *Because she never lands!*

23. Why should you never call someone average?

a. Because it's mean.

24. What do you call a lot of killer whales playing musical instruments?

a. An orca-stra.

25. **What do you call a fake noodle?**

a. *An impasta.*

26. **What did Dad think of the paper-ripping job?**

a. *He said it was tearable.*

27.   Why shouldn't you kiss someone on January 1st?

a.   Because it's the first date!

28.   Why did the child get arrested for refusing to take a nap?

a.   Because she was resisting a rest.

29.   Where is the best place to buy broth?

a.   At the stock market.

30.   What does the dad do to deal with his kleptomania?

a.   He takes something for it.

31.   **What did the dad who was scared of elevators do?**

a.   *He took steps to avoid them.*

32.   **Why should you avoid the restaurant on the moon?**

a.   *Because it doesn't have a good atmosphere!*

33. How does a polar bear build its house?

a. *Igloos it together.*

34. Where does Bruce Wayne go to use the toilet?

a. *To the batroom.*

35. **Why did the dad spider tell his son to go outside and play?**

a. *Because he was spending too much time on the web!*

36. **How do you organize an event in outer space?**

a. *You planet.*

37.   Why did the dad stay home after eating seafood?

a.   Because he felt a little eel.

38.   Why was the skeleton so calm?

a.   Because nothing got under its skin.

39. **Which is the worst diet to lose weight on?**

a. The seafood diet. When you see food, and eat it.

40. **Why did the bicycle need help standing up?**

a. Because it was two-tired.

41.   Why was six afraid of seven?

a.   Because seven ate nine.

42.   Why did Dad get fired from the calendar factory job?

a.   Because he kept taking time off!

43.   Why do octopi always win in fights?

a.   Because they are well-armed.

44.   How do you know that all ants are girls?

a.   Because if any were boys they'd be uncles!

45. **Why did the banana put on sunscreen?**

a. *Because he didn't want to peel!*

46. **Hey Dad, is it safe to dive in the pool?**

a. *It deep ends.*

47. **What do you think of your job at the prison library?**

a. *It has prose and cons.*

48. **Do cow mothers like coffee?**

a. *Yes, but they prefer de-calf.*

49. How did the dad feel about the boiling water that he lost?

a. He mist it!

50. Why did the coffee call the police?

a. Because it got mugged.

51.   Why didn't the skeleton go to the dance?

a.   Because it had no body to go with!

52.   Did they finish fixing the office floor?

a.   No, but they're working on it.

53. **What do you call cheese that doesn't belong to you?**

a. *Nacho cheese.*

54. **Why did the dad put peanut butter in the road?**

a. *To go with the traffic jam.*

55. **Why do seagulls fly over the sea?**

a. Because if they flew over the bay they'd be bay-gulls!

56. **Why were people so excited when the shovel was invented?**

a. Because it was a ground-breaking invention.

57. **Why did the graveyard seem overcrowded?**

a. *Because people were dying to get in there!*

58. **What did Dad think about the all-almond diet?**

a. *He thought it was just nuts.*

59.   Why did the large cat get kicked out of the game?

a.   Because he was a cheetah.

60.   What does a grape do when you step on it?

a.   It wines a little.

61. **Why did the Energizer Bunny go to jail?**

a. Because he was charged with battery

62. **Why did the slug call the police?**

a. Because it was a-salted.

63. **Why did the graduate thank sidewalks in his graduation speech?**

a. *For keeping him off the streets.*

64. **Dad used to hate the idea of having a beard.**

a. *But then it grew on him.*

65.   Why do you never see anyone with a nose that's 12 inches long?

a.   Because then it would be a foot!

66.   What award did they give the guy who invented door knockers?

a.   The no-bell prize!

67.   How did Dad feel after running behind a truck all day?

a.   Exhausted!

68.   "Dad, I broke my arm in several places?"

a.   "You should stop going to those places."

69. **How was the book about glue?**

a. *Great! I couldn't put it down!*

70. **Did you hear about the kidnapping?**

a. *He's fine, he woke up eventually.*

71. **What did the fast tomato say to the slow tomato?**

a.   *"Catch up!"*

72. **What do you call a cow that doesn't have any legs?**

a.   *Ground beef.*

73. **What did the dad buffalo say when he dropped his son off at college?**

a. *Bison.*

74. **How many tickles does it take before you can make an octopus laugh?**

a. *Ten-tickles.*

75. Dad, why did you say there are only 25 letters in the English language?

a. *I don't know why.*

76. What is the best part about Switzerland?

a. *The flag is a big plus.*

77.   **How do you call someone in prison?**

a.   *Just use a cell phone!*

78.   **Why did the mathematician get fat?**

a. Because he ate too much pie?

79. **What is the name of the fattest knight?**

a. *Sir Cumference.*

80. **Why did Dad get rid of all the round plates?**

a. *Because no one was eating a square meal.*

81. How do you make sure the sea creature is playing the right song?

a.   You have to tuna fish.

82. What is the loudest pet there is?

a.   A trumpet.

83.   How did they get the confession out of the hamburger patty?

a.   They grilled him.

84.   What do you get when you cross Frosty the Snowman with Dracula?

a.   Frostbite.

85. **What do you call a blind deer?**

a. **No ideer.**

86. **Hey Dad, can February March?**

a. *No, but April May.*

87. **What do you call cheese without any friends?**

a. *Provolone.*

88. **Why is it impossible to hear a pterodactyl going to the bathroom?**

a. *Because the p is silent.*

89. **What did the vegetarian zombie say?**

a. *"GRAAAIIIIIIIIIIIINS!"*

90. **Why should you not get in a fight with a pepper?**

a. *Because it will get jalapeño face!*

91.   What should you call someone with no body and just a nose?

a.   Nobody knows.

92.   Where do immortal college students shop?

a.   Forever 21.

93.   Why did the singer carry a bucket with her?

a.   So she could carry a tune!

94.   Why do crabs never share?

a.   Because they're shellfish!

95. **Mom went through a tropical food craze. There was fruit all over the house.**

a. *It was enough to make a mango crazy.*

96. **What do you call it when a prisoner takes his own mugshot?**

a. *A cellfie.*

97. **The wedding I went to was so touching.**

a. *Even the cake was in tiers!*

98. **Where do you go to make dessert?**

a. *In sundae school.*

99.   What did you think of the two antennas' wedding?

a.   The ceremony wasn't much, but the reception was great!

100.   Why should you never trust atoms?

a.   Because they make up everything.

Made in the USA
San Bernardino, CA
16 December 2019